BRIGHT
IDEA
BOOKS

HOW DO Cars DRIVE THEMSELVES?

Marcia Amidon Lusted

raintree

a Capstone company — publishers for children

Raintree is an imprint of Capstone Global Library Limited, a company incorporated in England and Wales having its registered office at 264 Banbury Road, Oxford, OX2 7DY – Registered company number: 6695582

www.raintree.co.uk
myorders@raintree.co.uk

Editor: Megan Gunderson
Designer: Becky Daum
Production Specialist: Colleen McLaren
Originated by Capstone Global Library Limited
Printed and bound in India

ISBN 978 1 4747 7529 8 (hardback)
22 21 20 19 18
10 9 8 7 6 5 4 3 2 1

ISBN 978 1 4747 7353 9 (paperback)
22 21 20 19 18
10 9 8 7 6 5 4 3 2 1

British Library Cataloguing in Publication Data
A full catalogue record for this book is available from the British Library.

Acknowledgements
AP Images: Bei Piao/Imaginechina, 18–19, Jose Juarez/Detroit News, cover (foreground), Philip Toscano/Press Association/URN: 30544691, 16–17, Uli Deck/picture-alliance/dpa, 11; Getty Images: Visual China Group, 5; iStockphoto: Chesky_W, 24–25, JasonDoiy, 14–15, 20–21, 28, 30–31, metamorworks, 22–23, zenstock, 6–7; Shutterstock Images: Grzegorz Czapski, 26, hxdyl, cover (background), metamorworks, 8–9, 13.
Design Elements: iStockphoto, Red Line Editorial, and Shutterstock Images.

We would like to thank Dr Jeffrey Miller at the University of Southern California for his invaluable help in the preparation of this book.

CONTENTS

CHAPTER 1

WHO'S Driving?

A car moves through city streets. It pauses for people crossing. It waits for a green light. Then it neatly parks near a shop.

Later the car heads for the motorway.
It merges smoothly with other cars. What is
so unusual? No one is driving it!

Self-driving cars don't need human drivers.
They steer themselves. Self-driving cars are
real. One day they will be a common sight.

Self-driving cars
hit the road!

ON THE WAY

Some cars are already partly self-driving. Many cars have cruise control. This keeps the car at a set speed.

Some cars also have special braking systems. They use **sensors** in the front. The sensors see when another car is too close.

If the system thinks there might be a crash, it uses the brakes. The car slows down and avoids a crash.

CRUISE

RES
+

CANCEL

−
SET

Cruise control keeps
a car's speed steady
without the driver's help.

In the future, a driver could decide whether to let the car drive itself.

No car is fully self-driving now. **Engineers** are working on cars that mostly drive themselves. The cars do most of the work. But they still need drivers to make some decisions.

Can we replace a human driver completely? Engineers are working hard to make this happen. Soon these cars of the future will be on the streets.

COMING SOON

Some companies are already designing self-driving cars. These include Tesla, Mercedes, BMW and Audi. Tech companies such as Google and Uber are making them too.

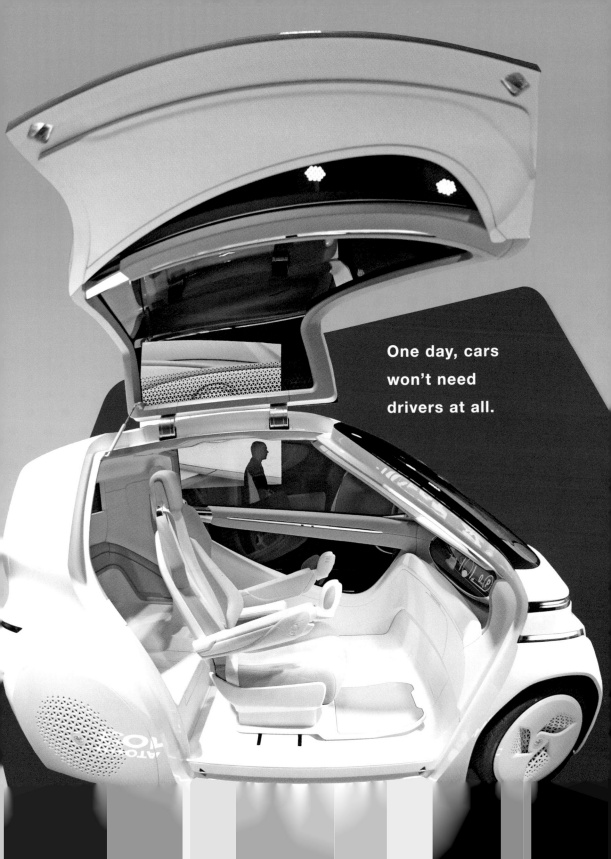

One day, cars won't need drivers at all.

CHAPTER 2

HOW IS IT
Driving?

How can engineers make a car drive itself? Computer systems must replace the driver. They must work together to drive the car.

LOOK OUT AHEAD

A driver must look out for objects ahead. A driverless car must do the same. Its sensors act as its eyes.

A self-driving car needs to sense everything around it.

These cars sense their surroundings with **lidar**. A lidar system looks like a bubble. It spins all the time.

Lidar uses lasers and scanners. Lasers bounce off nearby things. The system senses everything around the car. This way, the car avoids anything in its way.

Lidar usually sits on top of the car.

Self-driving cars also use **radar**. Radar uses radio waves. The waves bounce off objects. Computers measure the waves. They map everything around the car.

ARE WE THERE YET?

The car needs to know where it is. It also needs to know where to go. Computers store the car's maps. Some maps show where the car is going. Other maps show what is around the car.

The car also uses **GPS.** The GPS network has satellites. The car uses the network to know where it is.

Maps and sensors allow drivers to take their hands off the steering wheel.

The computers put together all the information. They make a current map. They choose a route for the car to follow. They tell the car to brake, speed up and steer.

A car must be programmed to follow traffic laws.

IT'S THE LAW

The car must also follow traffic laws. The car's computers know the speed limits. They note special traffic conditions.

More importantly, the car must make decisions. Another car might drive through a red light. How will the self-driving car react? It must track the situation. It must decide when to brake.

WHERE'S THE STEERING WHEEL?

Totally self-driving cars will look different! The car will not need a steering wheel. It will not even need pedals on the floor.

CHAPTER 3

WHY GO
Driverless?

Why do we need self-driving cars? Today there are many problems with driving. People think these cars can help solve these problems.

There is still much to do before self-driving cars are safe and common.

STAY SAFE

Thousands of people die in traffic accidents every year. Self-driving cars will be safer than traditional cars.

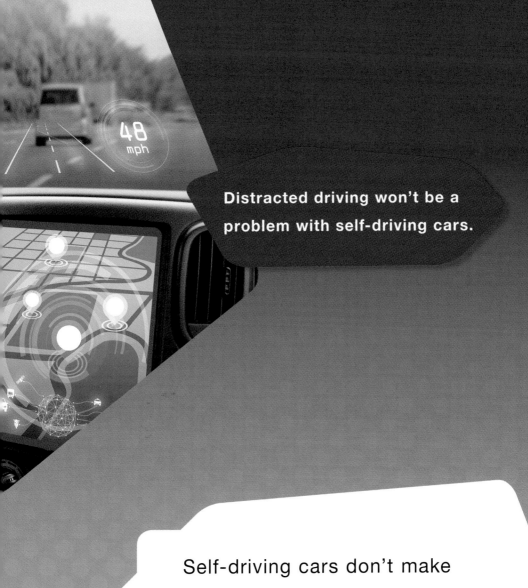

Distracted driving won't be a problem with self-driving cars.

Self-driving cars don't make mistakes like human drivers. They don't fall asleep while driving. They can see in all directions at the same time.

LET ME DRIVE YOU

Some people cannot drive. Self-driving cars will help them.

These cars will make it easier for people with **disabilities** to travel.

In a self-driving car, a driver could turn around to face the passengers.

Imagine what the cars of the future will look like!

SHARE THE ROAD

Self-driving cars can cut down on **pollution**. Many of these cars will be electric. They will harm our planet less.

Fewer cars would also help the planet. Some people hope self-driving cars will be shared more. Then there will be fewer cars on the road.

THE FUTURE

Self-driving cars are the cars of the future! They will be safer. They will help everyone get around. And they could be better for the planet. Those are very important reasons for designing and building them.

WE NEED YOU

It will take many clever people to create self-driving cars. That could be you in the future! Engineers at carmakers such as Jaguar Land Rover are testing self-driving cars. Universities have courses on developing them.

GLOSSARY

disability
a physical or mental condition that limits a person's ability to do various tasks

engineer
a person who designs, builds and fixes machines

GPS
(Global Positioning System) a system of satellites that can work out the position of a person or vehicle

lidar
a sensing system that uses light from a laser

pollution
substances that make land, water or air dirty, unsafe or unusable

radar
a sensing system that uses radio waves

sensor
a device that measures and responds to inputs like heat, motion, moisture or other conditions

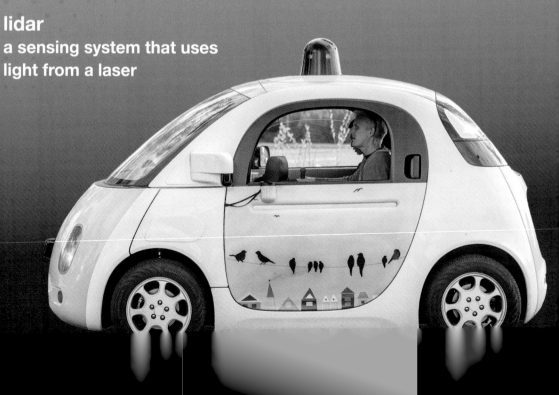

TRIVIA

1. Robotic taxis: The Nissan car company is testing self-driving taxis in Japan. These taxis will drive on preset routes. Passengers can use a phone app to call the taxi and pay for it.

2. Self-driving lorries: Self-driving lorries are already being tested. Lorries usually drive on long, straight roads. There are few twists and turns. These routes are easier for self-driving lorries.

3. Flying cars? The Uber company is testing flying cars. They will be similar to helicopters and drones. They will take off and land from rooftops. The cars are only for short trips, usually in cities. Eventually these cars will be self-driving.

ACTIVITY

Imagine you are an engineer. Design a car that drives itself. What special features does it have? How is it different from traditional cars?

Choose a place where you'd like the car to go. Draw a simple map from your home or school to that place.

Write a list of instructions for your driverless car based on your map. What does it have to do first? Which ways will it have to turn? When will it have to slow down or speed up? What does it have to look for, such as street signs or walkers? Make the list as complete as you can. Read your finished list out loud to a friend. Do the steps make sense to your friend? Have you left out anything?

EXTRA:

If you or your classroom have a robotics system that lets you build vehicles and program them (such as Lego Mindstorms), try programming your car to drive itself over your map.

FIND OUT MORE

Books

Car Science: A White-Knuckle Guide to Science in Action, Richard Hammond (DK Children, 2011)

Top Gear: Dream Cars: The Hot 100, Sam Philip (BBC Books, 2014)

Websites

BBC Earth Lab: How driverless cars work
www.youtube.com/watch?v=ZqRTVhiEill

A look at the UK's latest car technology
www.techworld.com/picture-gallery/startups/uks-top-car-tech-startups-3671300/

INDEX